THE
WATER CYCLE!

Anita Yasuda

Illustrated by Tom Casteel

Titles in the **Explore Earth Science** Set

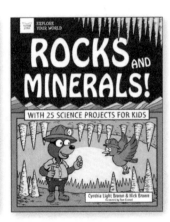
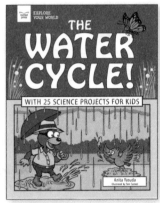

Check out more titles at www.nomadpress.net

Nomad Press

A division of Nomad Communications

10 9 8 7 6 5 4 3 2 1

This book was manufactured by Versa Press, East Peoria, Illinois
February 2020, Job #J19-11231
ISBN Softcover: 978-1-61930-870-1
ISBN Hardcover: 978-1-61930-867-1

Educational Consultant, Marla Conn

Questions regarding the ordering of this book should be addressed to
Nomad Press
2456 Christian St., White River Junction, VT 05001
www.nomadpress.net

Printed in the United States.

CONTENTS

Interested in primary sources? Look for this icon. Use a smartphone or tablet app to scan the QR code and explore more! Photos are also primary sources because a photograph takes a picture at the moment something happens.

You can find a list of URLs on the Resources page. If the QR code doesn't work, try searching the internet with the Keyword Prompts to find other helpful sources.

→ 🔍 EXPLORE WATER CYCLE

SNOW

The world's largest snowflake was 15 inches across and 8 inches thick! It was spotted in Montana on January 28, 1887.

GROUNDWATER

About 25 percent of all rainfall in the United States becomes groundwater.

OCEANS

The largest ocean on Earth is the Pacific Ocean. It covers about 30 percent of the earth's surface!

CLOUDS

A cloud might look fluffy and weightless, but even fair-weather clouds can weigh a million pounds.

RIVERS

Small rivers can have different names—creek, stream, brook, spring, crick, and more.

GLACIERS

About 69 percent of the world's fresh water can be found frozen in glaciers. We need to conserve water so there's plenty for everyone!

v

INTRODUCTION

LET'S EXPLORE WATER

Can you guess what I am? I have been here since Earth was first created. I splash and spill. I drip and drop. You cook with me, play in me, and drink me. I can run through your fingers, be hard as a rock, and become invisible. I flow through your body and history. I guide explorers and helped the first settlers to power their mills. Can you guess what I am? Water!

Water is amazing. One-quarter of all species live in the water. There would be no people in the past, present, or future without water. But we often take water for granted. And that's a mistake! We are very lucky to have water.

As far as we know, Earth is the only planet with liquid water on its surface. Let's see why water is so important.

WORDS ⊚ KNOW

species: a group of plants or animals that are closely related and produce offspring.

1

THE WATER CYCLE!

WORDS TO KNOW

water vapor: water in the form of a gas, such as steam or mist.

erosion: the wearing down of the earth's surface, usually by water, wind, or ice.

landform: a physical feature of the earth's surface, such as a mountain or a valley.

waterway: a channel of water, such as a stream or river.

glacier: a huge mass of ice and snow.

conservation: managing and protecting natural resources.

WATER IN THE BEGINNING

Imagine traveling through time to the beginning of the earth. Hop on our tour bus, leaving now for the very distant past! Take a look around. This is the earth more than 4 billion years ago. Of course, it looks very different from today.

Earth begins as a hot swirling mass of gas, rock, and dust. Later, these parts come together to form a huge glowing ball. Inside is water. As the earth's center heats up, water vapor rises to the surface. Get out your umbrellas! As the earth starts to cool, that water vapor turns into liquid—it's raining! For millions of years, it rains. Meanwhile, huge landmasses smash together like bumper cars and then split apart. The falling rain collects in the empty, low-lying areas. This is how oceans begin.

As the earth cools and warms, water freezes, thaws, and carves the surface. This is erosion. Eventually, the earth's land and water formations will begin to look familiar to you.

Do you think the earth's physical features are the same now as when you were born? They are not. Landforms and waterways, including the oceans, constantly change.

DID YOU KNOW?

The amount of water on Earth will remain the same forever. But water can spend a lot of time trapped in various places, such as in a glacier. That's why we practice water conservation, to make sure there's enough for everyone in the places it's needed.

OCEANS

Earth has one global ocean. Scientists and geographers divide this massive body of water into five different regions based on factors such as history, culture, and science. The five oceans are the Atlantic, Pacific, Indian, Arctic, and Southern Oceans.

culture: the beliefs and customs of a group of people.

resource: something found in nature that is useful to humans, such as water to drink, trees to burn, and fish to eat.

cargo: things carried by ship, truck, train, or airplane.

reservoir: a place that holds water.

continent: a large landmass.

WORDS ⊚ KNOW

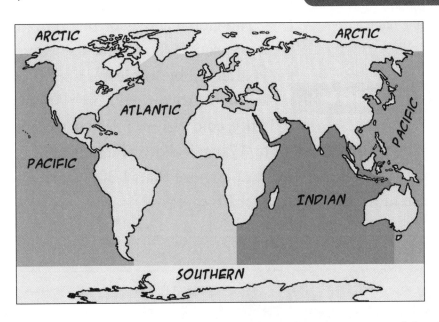

The oceans are full of resources. They are a source of food, energy, and materials such as salt and sand. They're also a highway for ships. For example, cargo ships carry billions of tons of goods every year. Oceans are fun to play in, too!

Oceans are the earth's largest water reservoirs. They cover about three-quarters of the earth's surface, or 140 million square miles. All seven continents could fit in the Pacific Ocean!

THE WATER CYCLE!

The global ocean is important for another reason. Have you ever been to the beach and watched the waves? Ocean water never stops moving. Tides, wind, waves, and currents keep the oceans constantly in motion. One large current shapes the earth's climate. It is called the global conveyor belt.

The global conveyor belt moves heat around the world. The current is affected by salt levels and temperature. In the North Atlantic, salty, cold water sinks, then travels south across the ocean floor. Warm surface water from the equator moves north. It can take more than 1,000 years for the water to move through the entire cycle!

Let's take a look at the three types of water on the planet.

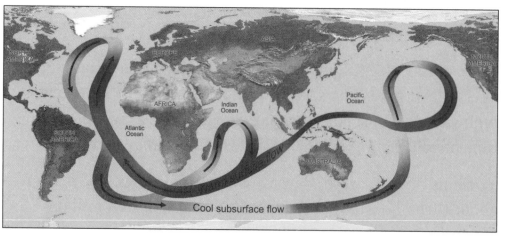

THE GLOBAL CONVEYOR BELT
CREDIT: NASA/JPL

minerals: naturally occurring solids found in rocks and in the ground.

ice cap: a thick layer of permanent ice.

WORDS ⊕ KNOW

SALT WATER

Have you ever seen a movie where people are floating in a lifeboat? When they drink water from the ocean, they quickly spit it out. *Yuck!* Why? Ocean water is just too salty for people. Most of the earth's water is undrinkable salt water—97 percent to be exact. But salt water is just right for many creatures. Birds, snails, and the largest animal on the planet, the blue whale, all call salt water home.

You can watch the global conveyor belt in action at this website. Can you see how this current affects the entire world?

⌐ THERMOHALINE CIRCULATION →

Why is the sea so salty? No one picked up a giant salt shaker and shook it into the ocean! When it rains, water flows over the land and picks up minerals. Salt is one of these minerals. Eventually, the water flows into the ocean. As time passes, the oceans get saltier and saltier. If you could spread ocean salt all over the earth, it would be more than 500 feet thick. That's the height of a 40-story building!

FRESH WATER

We all need fresh water to live. After playing outside, you grab a drink of water. *Glug, glug, glug.* You don't give it a second thought. But fresh water isn't as common as you think. Only 3 percent of all the water in the world is fresh. Most of this water is out of reach—in ice caps, glaciers, and underground. Only 1 percent of all fresh water is available for us to drink.

5

THE WATER CYCLE!

Where else can fresh water be found on our planet?

✳ Water vapor in the air

✳ Rain, snow, sleet, and hail

✳ Surface water such as rivers, lakes, ponds, and wetlands

✳ Groundwater from cracks and spaces underground

Rivers, streams, ponds, and lakes are freshwater ecosystems. But have you heard of prairie potholes? They are common in areas of western Canada and in the northern Great Plains.

Prairie potholes formed during the last ice age. When glaciers moved over the land, they created thousands of shallow wetlands. These wetlands, known as prairie potholes, fill with melted snow and rain in the spring. Many species of plants, animals, and insects rely on these temporary pools of water.

PRAIRIE POTHOLES IN NORTH DAKOTA
CREDIT: USFWS MOUNTAIN-PRAIRIE (CC BY 2.0)

ice sheet: a thick layer of ice covering a large area of land for a long time, especially those in Antarctica and Greenland.

rotation: a turn around a fixed point.

WORDS TO KNOW

FROZEN WATER

More than two-thirds of the earth's fresh water is frozen. Ice caps and glaciers hold the bulk of this water. Ice caps are permanent sheets of ice found around the North and South Poles. In the south, the Antarctic ice sheet is about 40 million years old. It rests on land. In the north, the Arctic ice cap floats on water. It rotates around the North Pole, taking four years to make one rotation.

Glaciers begin life as a snowflake. Unlike the snowflakes you catch on your tongue, these snowflakes don't melt. The layers upon layers of snow slowly turn to ice.

OUR BLUE PLANET

From space, the earth looks like a bright blue gumball! Looking closer, you can spot the five Great Lakes of North America, the dark lines of the Amazon River, and the bright blue of the oceans. No matter where you look, you see water. This is not surprising, because water covers 71 percent of earth. It is in the puddles on your street and in the streams near your home. Water is even in the air.

THE EARTH
CREDIT: NASA/GSFC/NOAA/USGS

For hundreds of years, this ice, along with sediment and rock, press together and form a glacier.

Glaciers are found on every continent except Australia. Most are found in Greenland and Antarctica. Alaska has thousands of glaciers, some the size of a football field and others that are miles long!

Time to put on your hydrologist hat! A hydrologist is a person who studies water. In the following pages, you'll read about the water cycle, rain harvesting, water power, water technology, and how to use water wisely.

CLIMATE CHANGE

Earth's climate is changing. Climate change is mostly caused by human activities. For example, when fossil fuels are burned in power plants or in cars, they release gases into the atmosphere that trap heat close to the earth's surface. Rising temperatures impact the water cycle. Warmer air holds more precipitation, which can lead to drought and flooding. There is a greater chance of severe storms. Warmer temperatures also cause glaciers to melt faster, leading to higher sea levels.

PS To learn more, check out Climate Kids.

— — — — — — →

🔎 CLIMATE KIDS

THE BERING GLACIER IN ALASKA IS THE LARGEST GLACIER IN NORTH AMERICA. IT IS 118 MILES LONG! CREDIT: NASA EARTH OBSERVATORY

You'll also discover how much water there is on Earth and why it falls from the sky. Along the way, you're going to do lots of fun projects, play games, do experiments, and hear some silly jokes. Be warned, though, you're going to get very wet as you drip, drop, splish, and splash around.

Ready? Let's explore water!

WHO LIVES WHERE?

Do you know which animals live in salt water or fresh water? Test your knowledge. For each of the following animals, write down whether they live in salt water or fresh water.

* emperor penguin
* crocodile
* hippopotamus
* gray whale

Now, research with an adult to find out if you're right.

GOOD SCIENCE PRACTICES

Every good scientist keeps a science journal! Choose a notebook to use as your science journal. Write down your ideas, observations, and comparisons as you read this book.

For your experiments, make and use a scientific method worksheet, like the one shown here. Scientists use the scientific method to keep their experiments organized. A scientific method worksheet will help you keep track of your observations and results.

Each chapter of this book begins with a question to help guide your exploration of water.

Scientific Method Worksheet

Question: What are we trying to find out? What problem are we trying to solve?

Research: What information is already known?

Hypothesis/Prediction: What do I think the answer will be?

Equipment: What supplies do I need?

Method: What steps will I follow?

Results: What happened? Why?

? INVESTIGATE!

What are some differences between fresh water and salt water?

Keep the question in your mind as you read the chapter. Record your thoughts, questions, and observations in your science journal. At the end of each chapter, use your science journal to record your thoughts and answers. Does your answer change as you read the chapter?

PROJECT!

WATER FORMS

SUPPLIES

✳ CD/DVD storage case
✳ modeling clay in assorted colors
✳ string
✳ scissors
✳ clear tape

Landforms and water cover the surface of the earth. They create the overall shape of the earth. Try this activity and make a clay water form. Here are some of the most common water forms.

- **River:** a small body of flowing water.

- **Bay:** an area of water surrounded by land on three sides.

- **Lake:** a large body of water, usually fresh water.

- **Strait:** a narrow body of water between two pieces of land. It joins two larger bodies of water.

- **Ocean:** the salty water that covers most of the earth's surface.

1 Choose a water form. Look in books or online for images. The U.S. Geological Survey website has a water science photo gallery here.

🔎 WATER USGS

2 Open a CD case. The bottom half will be your base. Thinly cover your base with one color of modeling clay.

3 Select a contrasting color to create a water form. Add clay fish and plants. Close the CD case. Attach the string with tape to the back and hang up your water form.

TRY THIS! You can repeat this experiment with a deeper container, such as a cake tin, and add water to it. Start a scientific method worksheet. What will happen if you blow on the surface of the water? Where will the water go? What will happen to the land? Try and see. Record your results in your science journal.

CHAPTER 1

W IS FOR WATER

You probably have lots of experience with water. You drink it, bathe in it, cook with it, and watch it drip off the roof when it rains. But what exactly is water?

Just like everything else in the world, water is made of matter. Inside matter are teeny tiny building blocks called atoms. You cannot see atoms, even with a powerful microscope. They are so small that they can't be cut in half. Until 1905, we didn't even have proof that atoms existed.

? INVESTIGATE!

How does water change from a solid to a liquid to a gas?

How many atoms do you think are in a glass of water? The exact number is hard to figure out. Imagine counting all the stars in the universe. That would be an enormous number! Well, a glass of water has more atoms in it than the universe has stars! *Atomazing!*

WATER MAGIC

There is nothing in the word like water. Water is odorless, tasteless, and colorless—and it's the most important substance on Earth. All living things need water to live.

Water exists in three different forms—solid, liquid, and gas. Water can transform from one form to another and then back again. It's like magic!

matter: any material or substance that takes up space.

atom: the smallest particle of matter.

hydrogen: the most common element in the universe, and one of the elements of water.

oxygen: an element that is a gas in the air. People and animals need oxygen to live.

element: a substance that contains only one kind of atom.

WORDS ⊙ KNOW

⋯ DID YOU KNOW? ⋯

The word *hydrologist* comes from the ancient Greek words *hydro* for "water" and *logos* for "study."

WATER MOLECULE CHEER

When atoms join, they form molecules. A water molecule is made of three atoms. And what are those three atoms?

Give me an H! . . . Give me a 2! . . . Give me an O!

What does that spell? . . . H_2O!

H stands for **hydrogen**. The number 2 means there are two hydrogen atoms. O stands for **oxygen**. Hydrogen and oxygen are two **elements**.

But water doesn't really transform because of magic. It needs a change in temperature to help it along. When the temperature drops below freezing, liquid water starts to turn into ice. When the temperature rises, the ice melts and becomes a liquid. And when the temperature gets really hot, water turns into a gas!

BRRRRRR: SOLID WATER

Almost 2 percent of all the earth's water is in the form of ice and snow. Glaciers and ice sheets lock in water. The largest ice sheet in the world covers the continent of Antarctica. This ice sheet holds 90 percent of the earth's fresh water!

THE VIEW FROM THE AIR OF THE VATNAJÖKULL GLACIER, ICELAND'S LARGEST GLACIER
CREDIT: NASA

dense: tightly packed.

molecule: a group of atoms.

WORDS to KNOW

Like an ice cube floating in a drink, parts of some glaciers and ice sheets float in the ocean. Have you ever wondered why an ice cube floats? Water becomes less dense when it freezes. When water freezes, its molecules expand. When other substances freeze, their molecules squish together like jellybeans in a jar.

Frozen water is less dense than liquid water, so it floats.

Frozen water doesn't move, but its molecules do—we just can't see them moving. It is much easier to see water moving when it is a liquid.

What happens when you pour water into containers with different shapes? The water quickly takes the shape of each container. Liquid water can bend and twist forward and back, until it fills every space!

A BLOCK OF ICE
CREDIT: BLUE LOTUS (CC BY 2.0)

THE WATER CYCLE!

greenhouse gas: a gas in the atmosphere that traps heat.

WORDS ⊕ KNOW

GASEOUS WATER!

When a pot of water boils on the stove, what do you notice about it? How did all those little bubbles get there? Those bubbles are water as a gas.

When water heats up, its molecules start to move very, very fast. They zoom and zip and spread out into the air, where they become water vapor—a gas.

Water vapor is a **greenhouse gas** and very important to the earth. A greenhouse gas traps heat. When water vapor traps heat, the earth's temperature rises. The average temperature here on Earth is 59 degrees Fahrenheit (15 degrees Celsius). Scientists believe that without water vapor, the average temperature would be a chilly 0 degrees Fahrenheit (-18 degrees Celsius)—too cold for life!

WATER VAPOR

WATER MOLECULES MOVING FASTER

HEAT SOURCE

LIQUID WATER

You are already familiar with liquid water—without it, you wouldn't be alive! One interesting property of liquid water is its stickiness. Sticky water? Yes!

Imagine you spilled a glass of water. You grab a paper towel and soak up the spill. The water moves up the paper towel. This is capillary action at work. Water molecules move into the spaces of other materials because of the way water molecules stick together.

capillary action: the way water pulls itself up into another material.

aquatic: living or growing in water.

surface tension: the force that holds the molecules together on the surface of a liquid, so that the liquid acts like it has a stretchy skin. Water has a high surface tension.

WORDS ᴛᴏ KNOW

(PS) You can see capillary action in this time-lapse video!

⌕ CAPILLARY ACTION HOREIN VIDEO

WATER'S SKIN

Can you walk across a pond? Probably not. But tiny **aquatic** insects called water striders can glide over water. **Surface tension** lets them do this! Here's how. Water molecules stick together. But water molecules at the surface have no molecules above them to cling to. So, they pull even tighter together. They pull so hard that a very thin "skin" forms. Water striders take advantage of this skin and glide across it.

THE WATER CYCLE!

gravity: a force that pulls all objects to the earth.

WORDS ⊚ KNOW

HOW DO YOU MAKE WATER?

You need everything from H to O!

Water molecules like to hang out together. This means they follow each other, even against gravity. "Okay, we are moving on up, guys," they seem to say as they travel up plant roots or fill in the spaces of a paper towel. If water molecules didn't like to stick together, there would be no raindrops. Instead, water would simply spread out.

?

CONSIDER AND DISCUSS

It's time to consider and discuss: How does water change from a solid to a liquid to a gas?

Now that we've refreshed our memories on the different forms of water, let's take a closer look at the water cycle in the next chapter!

THEN & NOW

THEN: Dowsing is a type of fortune-telling used to find underground water. A dowser walks over an area of land with a Y-shaped stick. A twitching stick is said to show the location of water. This method used to be popular.

NOW: Today, scientists locate groundwater by studying the landscape. They look for clues in the minerals and soil. Water-loving plants such as willow trees are also important clues.

CHANGE YOUR STATE

Try this game to act like a water molecule! What can you learn about how water behaves by copying it?

In this game, you and your friends are water molecules. One person plays the scientist. The other players must reach the scientist before getting out.

1 All the water molecules form a line at least 15 feet away from the scientist. The scientist faces away from the line and says, "Liquid." Each player must link arms with one other player and move toward the scientist.

2 The scientist may then say, "Solid," count to five, and turn around. Players must link arms with at least four others and shake. If the scientist sees any players not in a group of at least five, they are out.

3 Play resumes when the scientist turns back around and says, "Liquid" or "Gas." Gas means that the temperature is rising quickly. Players must spread out in all directions.

4 The scientist wins if all the players are out before anyone can touch the scientist. Otherwise, the first player to touch the scientist wins the game and is the scientist for the next game.

TRY THIS! First, review the main stages in the water cycle. Next, choose one person to go first. This person will pretend to be a water molecule in a stage of the water cycle. Like in charades, this person may only use hand or body movements. The person who guesses the stage correctly gets to go next.

PROJECT!

WHICH IS FASTER?

Try this experiment to investigate how molecules move in hot and cold water. Write down a prediction in your scientific journal. Will the cup with hot or cold water leak fastest? Why?

1 With the pin, poke a hole in the bottom of the paper cups. Balance each cup inside a glass.

2 Fill one cup with ice water and the other with very hot water.

3 Which cup leaks water faster? Write down your observations and add diagrams in your science journal.

4 Compare your results with your prediction. How could you make the water move more quickly or more slowly? Write down your ideas in your science journal.

TRY THIS! Test the movement of hot and cold water molecules with food dye. Fill one glass with hot water and another glass with ice water. Before you add the food coloring, write a prediction in your science journal. Which food coloring will spread faster? Add a drop of red food dye to the hot water and a drop of blue food dye to the cold water. Do not stir. What happens to the food coloring? Compare your results to your prediction.

WORDS ⊚ KNOW

diameter: the distance across a circle through the middle.

20

CLIMBING WATER

SUPPLIES

* science journal and pencil
* 2 glasses
* water
* paper towel

Try this experiment to see water move uphill and down. It's not magic—it's capillary action! Plants use capillary action to move water from their roots to their leaves.

1 Place two glasses on a table and fill one three-quarters full of water. Leave the other glass empty.

2 Write down a prediction in your scientific journal. How long do you think it will take for the water to empty out of the glass?

3 Twist a paper towel tightly and place one end in the glass with water and the other end in the empty glass.

4 Check on the glasses several times during the next few hours. Write down your observations and add diagrams in your science journal.

5 Compare your results with your prediction. How could you make the water move more quickly? Try it and see.

TRY THIS! What other objects in your house would allow water to climb by capillary action? Write down your ideas in your science journal. Then, try one and see what happens.

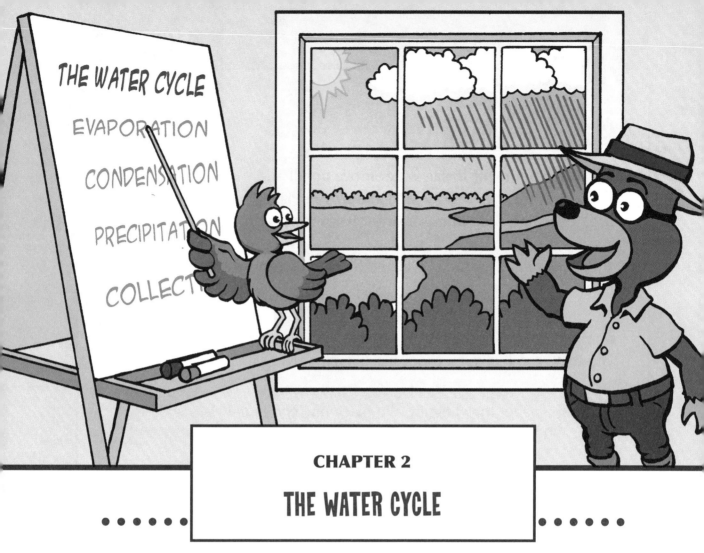

CHAPTER 2

THE WATER CYCLE

Earth's water is always moving. It moves between the air, the land, and the oceans. This movement is called the water cycle. The water cycle is everywhere! Water constantly circulates as a solid, liquid, or gas. Where does water come from and where does it go? Under the ground! Into the air! Over the land! All these answers are correct.

The total amount of water on Earth and in the atmosphere does not change. It has not changed since before dinosaurs roamed the earth. While the amount of water stays the same, the form that this water takes does change—a lot!

 INVESTIGATE!

What are clouds made of?

Learn more about how water is recycled on Earth at this website.

🔍 CRASHCOURSE DINOSAUR PEE

→

evaporation: the process by which a liquid becomes a gas.

condensation: the process by which a gas cools and forms a liquid.

precipitation: water that falls back to the earth's surface as rain, snow, or hail.

collection: the process by which water that falls back to the earth is stored on land or in oceans, ponds, rivers, lakes, and streams.

aquifer: an underground layer of rock that has space in it that holds water.

WORDS ⓣⓞ KNOW

The water cycle does not have a beginning or an end. Instead, the earth's water is always being recycled. It moves through a series of four major processes—evaporation, condensation, precipitation, and collection.

Earth's water works its way through the cycle at different speeds. Water spends only a short time in the air as rain or snow. Water in lakes may take decades to cycle. Water in oceans, glaciers, and some aquifers can take thousands of years to cycle.

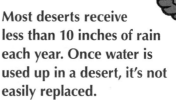

⋯ DID YOU KNOW? ⋯

Most deserts receive less than 10 inches of rain each year. Once water is used up in a desert, it's not easily replaced.

And water in deserts, which receive little or no precipitation, could take a million years to cycle!

Let's take a look at the different stages of the water cycle.

HOW DID THE SNOWMAN GET TO SCHOOL?

By icicle!

FALLING HAMBURGER BUNS!

What do raindrops look like? Do they have pointy tops and round bottoms? No! They look like hamburger buns and beans. The smallest raindrops, less than 0.01 inch across, are round spheres. Medium-sized raindrops, about 0.12 inches, look like beans. Anything bigger than 0.2 inches resembles a hamburger bun. Next time it rains, spread a thin layer of baking grease on a cookie sheet and catch a few raindrops on it. The raindrops will make holes in the grease. Check out their shapes!

EVAPORATION: It's raining, and puddles form all around the playground. At recess, the sun comes out, and the puddles start to disappear. The heat of the sun causes water to evaporate. The water molecules have become a gas.

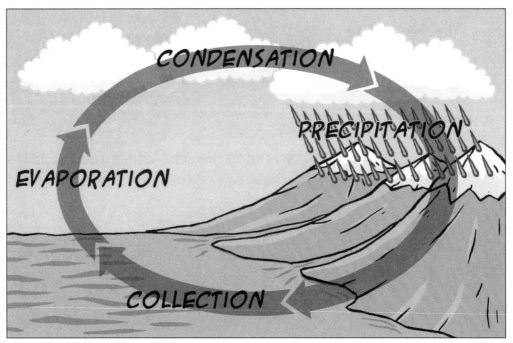

Water evaporates at all temperatures. But heat causes water molecules to evaporate faster. Think about the water inside a kettle. When the kettle is heated, the water boils. Soon, you see steam flowing from the spout. The water inside a kettle of boiling water evaporates faster than the water in the puddles.

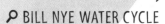

Watch this video to learn even more about the water cycle.

🔍 BILL NYE WATER CYCLE

CONDENSATION: There's nothing like a cold glass of water on a hot day! Have you ever noticed the tiny drops of water on the outside of a glass? Is it leaking? No, these tiny drops are

water vapor. The water vapor in the air cools when it touches the cold glass. It turns back into liquid water. This process is called condensation.

PRECIPITATION: Water vapor does not stay in the air long. As it rises, it cools into water droplets through condensation. It may turn into ice crystals at higher and colder levels. These ice droplets or crystals bump and stick together. They grow larger until they form a cloud. Each cloud contains millions of droplets!

WORDS TO KNOW

runoff: the flow of water that drains off an area of land.

adapt: to make a change in response to new or different conditions.

In about 12 days or less, the droplets or crystals fall as precipitation in the form of rain, snow, or hail. On average, 0.8 inches of rain falls on Earth each day. Most of this precipitation falls in the oceans. The rest falls on the land, where it then takes various paths back to the ocean. You will learn more about precipitation in Chapter 3.

COLLECTION: Where does water collect before it starts evaporating again? Most water goes into the ocean. This isn't surprising, since oceans cover more than 70 percent of the earth. Water also flows over land into lakes, rivers, and streams as runoff.

DID YOU KNOW?

If all the water under the ground was spread over the earth's surface, it would be 180 feet deep.

EXTREME PLANTS

All living things need water. Have you ever wondered how plants in deserts get water? Plants soak up water with their roots when it rains. But some deserts, such as the Atacama in Chile, do not receive rain for years. The Atacama Desert is the driest desert on Earth. To survive there, plants soak up dew or fog. They trap the moisture from the Pacific Ocean on their leaves or spines. These plants have **adapted** to live in a region with very little rainfall.

(PS) **Read more about the Atacama Desert here.**

𝒫 KIDDLE ATACAMA

unsaturated zone: an area below ground that has water and air between rocks.

saturated zone: an area below ground filled with water.

WORDS ⊕ KNOW

Some precipitation soaks into the ground, where it becomes groundwater. This is one source of our drinking water. Water first enters the soil in what's called the unsaturated zone. This area is full of dirt and air. Some of the water that collects here is used by plants.

The rest of the water goes deeper, into the saturated zone, which is filled with water. Here, the water collects in cracks between rocks called aquifers. This water begins a very slow journey through the ground to the ocean. Eventually, all collected water evaporates and the water cycle begins again.

The water cycle means that water is very closely related to the kind of weather we experience. We'll take a closer look at that connection in the next chapter.

? CONSIDER AND DISCUSS

It's time to consider and discuss: What are clouds made of?

THEN & NOW

THEN: The ancient Egyptians stored water from the Nile River in large jars. They waited for the mud to settle out of the water before they drank it.

- - - - - - - - - - - - - - - -

NOW: In many countries, water travels through water treatment plants to make it safe to drink.

PROJECT!

BELL JAR TERRARIUM

Make a terrarium to see how the water cycle works. A terrarium is like a miniature Earth in a jar!

1 Clean and dry your jar and lid. Put soil, small stones, and moss at the bottom of the jar. Add a small plant to the soil.

2 Use the eyedropper to add a little water to the soil. The soil should be moist.

3 Screw the lid onto the jar and place your terrarium in a sunny spot.

> **⋯ DID YOU KNOW? ⋯**
>
> **Dew appears on grass on cool mornings because water in the air condenses as the temperature falls overnight. Where does the dew go? As the temperature rises, the dew evaporates back into the air.**

4 During the next few days, write down your observations in your journal. What happens to the jar? What happens to the plant?

TRY THIS! How does the amount of water you add to the jar affect the experiment? Write down a prediction in your science journal. Then, repeat this experiment using more or less water.

WORDS TO KNOW

terrarium: a sealed, transparent container in which plants are grown.

dew: water droplets made when humid air cools at night.

SUPPLIES

✳ leafy potted plant
✳ clear plastic bag
✳ scissors
✳ measuring cup

PROJECT!

TRANSPIRATION

Plants carry water from their roots to their leaves. Some of this water is then released into the air through tiny pores called stomata. **This process is called** transpiration. **See how transpiration works in this experiment.**

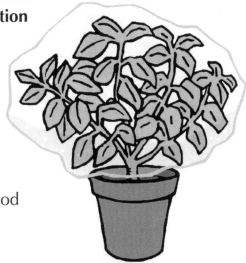

1 Cover the leaves of the leafy potted plant with a plastic bag.

2 How much water will the bag collect in a day? Write down a prediction on your scientific method worksheet.

3 During the next few hours write down your observations. The following day, check the bag.

4 Cut off a corner of the bag and allow the water to drain into the measuring cup.

5 Compare your results with your prediction.

6 Add your results and diagrams to your science journal.

TRY THIS! Do you think plants such as evergreens or cacti would have more or less transpiration than a leafy potted plant? Write down a prediction in your science journal. Try and see.

WORDS ⊕ KNOW

stomata: the tiny openings on plant leaves for air to enter.

transpiration: the process by which a plant pulls water up through its roots, which then collects on its leaves and evaporates into the atmosphere.

PROJECT!

WATER CYCLE BAND

Wear the water cycle on your wrist!

SUPPLIES

* ✳ toilet paper roll
* ✳ scissors
* ✳ paint brush
* ✳ light green paint
* ✳ yellow, dark blue, silver, white, and light blue circle stickers or bingo markers

1 Cut the paper roll along one length and then cut the roll in half width-wise. Place the extra half to one side.

2 Using the paint brush, paint the outside of the bracelet green. The green represents the land and the plants. Wait for the paint to dry.

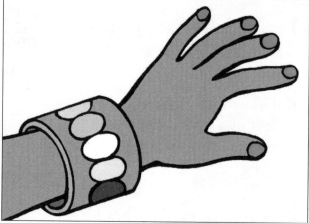

3 Create a pattern around your bracelet with stickers or bingo markers in this order: yellow, silver, white, light blue, and dark blue. Each color represents a stage in the water cycle.

* Yellow=sun
* Silver=evaporation
* White=condensation
* Light blue=precipitation
* Dark blue=collection

4 Wear your bracelet to remember the different stages of the water cycle.

TRY THIS! Make another bracelet of the water cycle with drawings of lakes, streams, clouds, and the sun. Add labels to your pictures.

CHAPTER 3

WATER AND WEATHER

**What's the weather like outside right now?
Knowing what the weather will be makes it easier
to plan activities and choose clothing!**

The weather we have is directly related to the movement of water. Without water, there would be no weather. Water is part of the air we breathe, the clouds above us, the precipitation that falls— water is everywhere! Let's take a look.

 INVESTIGATE!

How are weather and water connected?

THE WATER CYCLE!

WORDS ᴛᴏ KNOW

humidity: the amount of moisture in the air.

WATER IN THE AIR

WHY DID THE WEATHER STATION CALL THE ANIMAL SHELTER?

It was raining cats and dogs!

On a warm day, laundry hangs on the clothesline. Will it dry? It depends on the humidity, the amount of moisture in the air.

Humidity changes all the time. High humidity means a lot of water is in the air. Your skin feels sticky. Low humidity means little water is in the air. Your skin is cool and dry. The laundry on the clothesline will dry more quickly when the humidity is low.

RAINFORESTS ARE KNOWN FOR BEING HUMID PLACES.

NAME THAT CLOUD

More than 200 years ago, Luke Howard (1772–1864) began studying clouds and the weather. At that time, clouds were not organized scientifically. People described clouds based on their looks—fluffy, white, or black. In 1802, Luke Howard published his weather observations. He placed clouds into three main groups, then later added a fourth group. The system is still used today!

* **Cirrus clouds** are thin, white, and wispy like feathers. Some people think they look like horse tails. They form high in the sky and usually mean good weather is on its way.

* **Nimbus clouds** are often dark gray. They can be so thick that they hide the sun. Watch out! They can mean that rain or snow is coming.

* **Cumulus clouds** are white and fluffy like cotton balls. They float low in the sky. They usually mean fair weather. But they can also grow and bring rain showers.

* **Stratus clouds** look like a gray, patched sheet across the sky. They are a sign that the weather is changing.

Remember the water cycle? Water spends some of its time in the atmosphere in the form of clouds. Clouds come in all shapes and sizes. That one looks like whipped cream! That one looks like a fish! All clouds are made of water droplets.

DID YOU KNOW?

Buildings and roads store heat during the day and lose it at night. When that warm air rises, it makes clouds. Scientists discovered that heat from cities impacts the weather. In the spring and summer, London and Paris have more cloud cover than the countryside.

As you know, most clouds form when water evaporates. The water vapor rises high into the sky and condenses into water droplets, which form clouds.

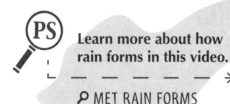

PS Learn more about how
rain forms in this video.

⌕ MET RAIN FORMS →

In the right conditions, the droplets fall as rain. If they pass through air that is below 32 degrees Fahrenheit (0 degrees Celsius), the droplets turn to snow.

Unlike snow, hail can fall in any temperature. Hail forms in thunderclouds where the water droplets constantly move up and down. As they move up, they become covered with ice. The more the droplets move up and down, the more ice attaches to them. When the cloud cannot hold them any longer, they fall as hail.

DID YOU KNOW?

The largest piece of hail in the United States fell in Vivian, South Dakota, on July 23, 2010. It was as large as a baseball and weighed nearly 2 pounds.

WEATHER TOOLS

Since ancient times, people have relied on their eyes to predict the weather. They looked for changes in nature such as flowering plants or budding trees. They closely watched animal behavior for clues. For example, some birds fly away before the weather turns cold.

The invention of weather tools made it possible to measure the weather using science. A **barometer** measures pressure in the air. High pressure usually means fair weather and low pressure means that rain is on its way.

An **anemometer** measures wind speed. Wind speed can indicate a change in the weather.

THUNDERSTORMS

We need meteorologists to accurately predict storms, but you can figure out how far away a storm is yourself. When you see a lightning flash, start counting the seconds. Stop when you hear thunder. Divide the number of seconds by five. That's about how many miles the thunderstorm is from you. The lightning and thunder occur at the same time, but light travels much faster than sound. So, you see the lightning before you hear the thunder.

THE WATER CYCLE!

THEN: The ancient Greeks believed the god Zeus controlled the weather.

NOW: We know that weather is influenced by the water cycle.

THEN & NOW

Today, we also have weather balloons that float up into the atmosphere. The weather balloons carry more tools, such as radiosondes, which record measurements about what's happening up there and then fall back to the earth, where scientists find them and use those measurements to study the weather even more.

Radar is another important tool in meteorology. Have you ever seen a weather radar map? Powerful instruments can show where precipitation is happening and where it might go next.

Scientists who study and predict the weather are called meteorologists. They measure changes in temperature and air pressure and use this information to make weather forecasts. We use this information to plan our day!

Besides giving us weather, what else does water do? For one thing, it helps humans by making power! We'll learn more in the next chapter.

CONSIDER AND DISCUSS

It's time to consider and discuss: How are weather and water connected?

PROJECT!

WEATHER SYMBOLS

Meteorologists forecast the weather. They represent it using symbols. In this activity, you can create symbols for weather events and use them in a weather forecast.

1 Write the weather words listed below in your science journal. Using colored pencils, draw a weather symbol beside each word.

Drizzle   Rain   Snow   Thunder   Fog   Freezing rain

2 Using your weather symbols, create an imaginary weather forecast in your science journal. Share your forecast with a friend.

WHAT KIND OF METEOR CAN TELL THE WEATHER?

A meteorologist!

3 Create a weather report based on the actual weather in your area. Start by making a bar graph in your science journal. Use the graph to record the weather where you live during a two-week period. Write the numbers from 0 to 14 along the left of the graph. The numbers represent the days. Along the bottom of the graph write the words "sun," "rain," "wind," "cloud," and "snow." Assign a color to each type of weather.

THINK ABOUT IT: What type of weather was most common? Why do you think this was?

METEOROLOGIST JOURNAL

SUPPLIES

* 10 to 15 sheets of recycled paper
* ruler
* pencil
* scissors
* pencil crayons
* hole punch
* 2 metal D rings

Make an earth-friendly journal out of recycled paper such as old graph paper, used envelopes, and other scraps. Then, record your weather observations in the journal.

1 Stack the paper and decide on a journal size.

2 Using a ruler, pencil, and scissors, cut the paper to the same size.

3 Choose one piece for your cover and draw pictures of different weather events, such as sunshine or rain.

4 Punch holes at the top and bottom of one side of the paper stack. Insert D rings into the holes.

5 During a month, record the weather. How warm is it when you get up each morning? Is it snowing or raining? What do the clouds look like? Draw pictures of these different weather events.

6 At the end of the month, read through your journal. What weather patterns do you see?

TRY THIS! Do you see any connections between the clouds in the sky and the weather that happens that day? Keep track of your observations to see if the cloud formations really do offer hints about what the weather is going to be.

PROJECT!

HAIR HYGROMETER

SUPPLIES

* plastic folder
* scissors
* ruler
* a strand of hair
* tape
* cardboard
* tack
* marker
* hair dryer

In 1783, scientist Horace Benedict de Saussure (1740–1799) invented the hygrometer**, which used human hair to measure humidity. Humid air makes hair stretch while dry air makes it shrink. Try it out!**

1 From the plastic folder, cut out an arrow pointer 1½ inches wide by 7 inches long. Tape one end of the hair to the flat end of the pointer, 1 inch from the edge. Tape the other end of the hair to the top of the cardboard so it hangs down.

2 Attach the pointer to the cardboard with a tack, one-half inch from the edge. The tack should fit loosely so the pointer moves.

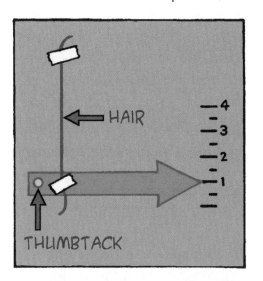

3 Draw a 4-inch scale so that the pointer lines up with the 1-inch mark.

4 With a hair dryer set on low, blow air on the hair for a few seconds and watch what happens.

5 Bring your hygrometer into a steamy bathroom. What happens?

TRY THIS! Make hygrometers with hair from different family members. Do you think the results will be different?

WORDS ᴛᴏ KNOW

hygrometer: an instrument that measures humidity.

PROJECT!

SUPPLIES

* ✳ science journal and pencil
* ✳ tape measure
* ✳ string
* ✳ 8 garden pegs
* ✳ black sand (available at a craft store)

SNOWPACK EXPERIMENT

During the winter, snow and ice build up in cold areas, creating a snowpack. The snowpack melts when temperatures rise. As the world gets warmer, the snowpack is melting earlier, which impacts our water supplies, plants, and animals. In this experiment, you will explore the snowpack melt. This is a winter project! Choose a week with no new snow in the forecast.

1 In your science journal, write down a prediction. Which do you think will melt faster: the white snow or the snow covered in black sand? Why?

2 Use the tape measure to create two equal square, plots of snow. Push the garden pegs into the snow at each corner. Tie the string between the pegs to create two squares.

3 Sprinkle a thin layer of black sand over one of the plots.

4 During a week, return to your plots. Record your observations in your science journal. Which plot melted faster and why do you think this was? Do you notice any other differences between the two plots?

WHAT IS HAPPENING? Black sand absorbs more heat from the sun than white snow.

TRY THIS! Next time it snows, capture snowflakes on black posterboard. Use a magnifying glass to examine the snowflakes outside. What do you notice about the snowflakes?

PROJECT!

MAKE A NILOMETER

SUPPLIES

✳ 6 plastic bottle caps, each 1½ inches high
✳ waterproof glue
✳ permanent marker
✳ ruler
✳ plastic container
✳ waterproof marker
✳ scissors
✳ fishing wire

In ancient Egypt, the Nile River was the main source of water. Every year the river would flood. To find out if the flood was going to be light, normal, or heavy, the Egyptians built a nilometer by the river. The nilometer looked like a staircase, with measurements written on the steps. Make a rain gauge inspired by a nilometer.

1 Glue the bottle caps to form a staircase. When the glue is dry, use a marker to make marks every quarter inch on each cap.

2 Glue the base of the staircase to the bottom of the inside of the container. With scissors, make two holes in the top of the container, one on each side.

3 Thread fishing wire through the holes and secure the container to a fence.

4 After each rainfall, check the level of the water. Record your measurements in your journal. Then, empty your nilometer so it's ready for the next rainfall.

TRY THIS! To make a simpler version of a rain gauge, cut off the top of a plastic bottle or use a wide-mouth mason jar. Using a ruler and a permanent marker, mark several measurements from the bottom to the top. Set your bottle on a flat surface outside. Record your measurements after each rainfall in your journal.

WORDS ᴛᴏ KNOW

nilometer: a device used in ancient Egypt to measure the height of water reached by the Nile during its annual floods.

41

CHAPTER 4

WATER WORKS

Since ancient times, people have wanted and needed to control water. Too little water could turn land to dust. Too much water could cause terrible destruction. For cities and towns to grow, a reliable source of fresh water was essential.

How did people figure out ways to control water? Read on to discover the tools and structures they used!

INVESTIGATE!

What are some ways humans control water?

AQUEDUCTS AND CISTERNS

Water is always on the move, but it doesn't always go where you want it to go. To control the flow of water, ancient civilizations in the Middle East built underground irrigation tunnels called qanats. The qanats moved water from mountain streams to fields and villages.

The ancient Romans built enormous structures called aqueducts to control the flow of water. Some aqueducts bridged valleys and rivers to bring water to Roman towns.

irrigation: a system of transporting water through canals or tunnels to water crops.

qanat: an underground water tunnel.

aqueduct: a network of channels used to move water across long distances.

WORDS ⊙ KNOW

(PS) **Watch this video to learn more about qanats.**

⌐ − − − − − − →

🔎 NAT GEO QANAT VIDEO

ANCIENT ROMAN AQUEDUCTS IN MODERN-DAY SPAIN

THE WATER CYCLE!

DID YOU KNOW?

Modern-day Tunisia was once part of the Roman Empire. Here, Romans used their engineering skills to build one of the longest aqueducts in their empire. It stretched for 80 miles!

All this water couldn't be used at once. It was stored in huge underground wells called cisterns. Cisterns were also used to collect rainwater. The Basilica Cistern in what is now Istanbul, Turkey, was built in 532 CE. The cistern was so large that it could hold more than 2 million cubic feet of water. Small boats could navigate between its pillars!

THE SHADUF

Ancient Egyptians depended on the Nile River for water. Every so often, the river flooded its banks, leaving behind rich soil. Farmers grew crops in this soil. To water the plants, farmers used an invention called the shaduf.

BASILICA CISTERN
CREDIT: GRYFFINDOR

A shaduf looks like a giant seesaw, with a long wooden lever arm resting on a stand. One end of the arm has a weight, such as a heavy stone, and the other has a bucket. When one end goes up, the other goes down.

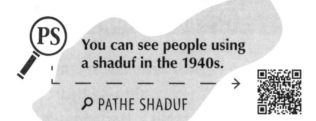

(PS) You can see people using a shaduf in the 1940s.

🔎 PATHE SHADUF →

To use the shaduf, farmers pulled the bucket down into the river. When the bucket was full, they released it. As the bucket rose, the weighted end dropped. This system works so well that farmers still use shadufs to water their crops in some parts of the world!

WATER WHEELS

An energy source that lasts forever is called renewable. This means we can't run out of it. Renewable energy is also healthier for the planet. Energy from the sun and wind is renewable. Moving water is another renewable source of energy.

People have been using moving water as a source of energy for hundreds of years. The ancient Greeks used the energy of water to move water wheels. These early wheels were made of wood. They had paddles attached to them. As moving water struck the paddles, the wheel turned. The wheels moved heavy stones inside mills, which ground grain into flour.

By the 1700s, power provided by water wheels was being used in fabric and lumber mills. Some of these water wheels were made of iron. Iron wheels were stronger than wooden wheels.

THE WATER CYCLE!

HYDROPOWER

In the nineteenth century, scientists learned how they could use hydropower to produce electricity. Hydropower uses moving water, especially waterfalls or fast-flowing rivers. In 1882, the world's first hydroelectric plant opened on the Fox River in Wisconsin.

··· DID YOU KNOW? ···

The largest hydroelectric plant in the United States is the Grand Coulee Dam in Washington state. The dam provides power for more than 2 million homes.

The energy of the Fox River forced blades within machines called turbines to spin. These turbines changed the energy into electricity. The electricity flowed along power lines. At first, the plant produced only enough electricity for the plant, a home, and a building nearby.

THE GRAND COULEE DAM, COLUMBIA RIVER BASIN, WASHINGTON STATE

dam: a large, strong wall built across a river to hold back and control the water.

generator: a machine that converts energy into electricity.

WORDS ⦿ KNOW

By the 1900s, hundreds of small hydropower plants were operating. Today, hydropower plants are all around the world, in all sizes. Many hydropower plants consist of a dam across a river. Water is held back behind the dam. As water is released through the dam wall, it spins the turbines. This creates electricity.

WATER ENERGY

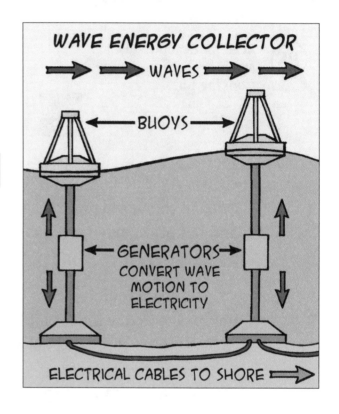

WAVE ENERGY COLLECTOR
→ ⟹ WAVES ⟹ →
←— BUOYS —→
←—GENERATORS—→
CONVERT WAVE MOTION TO ELECTRICITY
ELECTRICAL CABLES TO SHORE ⟹

Water acts as a source of energy in other ways, too. Ocean waves are a source of energy, but this energy is challenging to capture! Scientists have designed devices that float on the ocean surface and move up and down on the waves. The waves drive a generator that changes the energy of moving water into electricity. Other devices attached to cables at the sea bottom carry electricity to the shore.

In 2008, the first wave energy farm opened in Portugal using devices that float. These giant red tubes the size of railroad cars are connected by hinges. When waves move the hinges, a generator makes electricity. This electricity travels from the tubes along a cable at the bottom of the ocean to the shore.

Another way to harness energy from water is by using the tides. Each day, tides cause the sea level to rise and fall by the shore. Like waves, tides are a source of energy. Again, this energy can be hard to collect.

HOW DO OCEAN WAVES SAY HELLO?

They just wave.

(PS) **Read more about how machines harness energy from the tides.**

🔍 CLIMATE KIDS TIDES →

One of the world's largest tidal projects is being tested in the Bay of Fundy in Nova Scotia, Canada. The project uses turbine devices to generate electricity. The Bay of Fundy has the highest and strongest tides in the world. More than 160 billion tons of water flow in and out of the bay each day! Tidal energy from the bay has the potential to power about 3 million homes.

Water is incredibly important to our planet and to everything that lives here. So how can we keep that water clean and healthy?

? CONSIDER AND DISCUSS

It's time to consider and discuss: What are some ways humans control water?

THEN & NOW

THEN: In ancient Rome, a private citizen hired hundreds of men to fight fires with buckets of water.

NOW: There are more than 1 million firefighters in the United States. They fight fire with water and water-based foams.

PROJECT!

ARCHIMEDES' SCREW

Greek scientist Archimedes (288–212 BCE) invented a device to move water from a river to a farmer's field. This device—called the Archimedes' screw—is a tube with a large spiral inside. When you place the tube in water and turn it, the spiral pushes the water up. Try it!

1 Poke one end of the pipe cleaner through the straw to secure it. Wind the pipe cleaner around the straw to make the screw, keeping the spaces between the spirals even.

2 Tightly wrap a piece of acetate around the screw to make a cylinder. Secure it with tape. It should fit snugly, but the screw should still be able to turn.

3 Pour sugar into a bowl and insert your screw at an angle. Place another bowl below the top of your screw. Turn the screw, not the cylinder. What happens to the sugar? What happens to the lowest point and highest point of the spiral?

TRY THIS! Make an Archimedes' screw that lifts water using only clear plastic tubing, a water bottle, and tape. Test your design. Based on your results, make changes to your design and try again.

49

PROJECT!

MINI WATER WHEEL

In this activity, build a model of a water wheel. How much water will your model lift? Try it and see!

Caution: An adult must help with this activity.

1 Cut out a circle 3 inches in diameter from a plastic lid. Use waterproof markers to decorate the top of the circle.

2 On the underside, divide the circle into six even sections. Have an adult help you poke a hole through the center.

⋯ DID YOU KNOW? ⋯

Philo of Byzantium (350–320 BCE) was a Greek engineer who wrote about general mechanics. He is believed to be the first person to describe a vertical wheel that could lift water.

WATER WHEELS

In 1684, engineers in Marly, France, needed to build a water system that would carry water to the palaces of the king of France, Louis XIV. They built one of the largest water wheel systems. The system used 14 water wheels to raise the water roughly 500 feet. This is about the same height as a 46-story building! The water then traveled along an aqueduct to the palaces.

3 With an adult, hot glue a spool to the underside of circle. Be careful not to glue the hole.

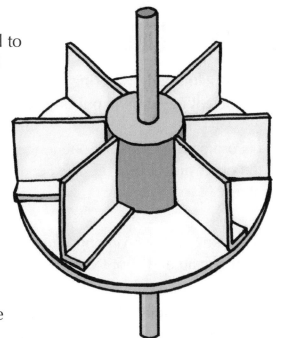

4 From the acetate or recycled plastic folder, cut out six tabs for paddles. They should measure about 1 inch by 1½ inches.

5 Bend the tabs slightly at the bottom. Hot glue them to the underside of the circle around the spool. Space them out evenly.

6 Push the straw through the spool and circle. The straw is the **axle**. It must move freely. Center your wheel on the straw.

7 Hold the water wheel under a trickle of water in a sink. Does your water wheel lift the water? Experiment with different strengths of flowing water.

TRY THIS! Make a stand for your water wheel to rest on. Make two notches on the opposite sides of a large plastic cup. You may have to ask an adult to help with this step. Rest the straw or axle on the notches. If the water wheel becomes unbalanced, secure the ends of the straw to the bottom of the sink with thread and masking tape.

WORDS ⊕ KNOW

engineer: a person who uses science, math, and creativity to design and build things.

axle: a rod on which a wheel rotates.

MAKE A SHADUF

The shaduf made watering crops easier for people in ancient Egypt. Find out how a shaduf worked.

1 Position the middle of one long stick in the V of the other stick, like a seesaw. Secure it with string and set it to one side.

2 Make two holes on opposite sides of the cup's rim. Leaving a long loop, thread and knot the string through the holes.

3 Tie the loop to one end of the long stick. Make the loop long enough so the cup can reach your water source.

DID YOU KNOW?

Scientists estimate that a person could raise approximately 2,500 liters of water a day using a shaduf. That's roughly 660 one-gallon milk jugs!

4 Tie another piece of string around the stone. Attach it to the other end of the stick. Leave enough length so that you can move the stone up and down the stick to balance the water.

5 Securely place the V stick in the ground near a water source. Try to collect water. If necessary, adjust the length of the string or its placement on the stick.

6 Write down your observations in your science journal and add diagrams. Does the weight of the cup change your experiment? Write down your ideas in your science journal. Try and see.

TRY THIS! Use shorter or longer sticks for the shaduf's lever. How will the length of the lever affect this experiment? Write down your ideas in your science journal. Try and see. Compare your result with your prediction.

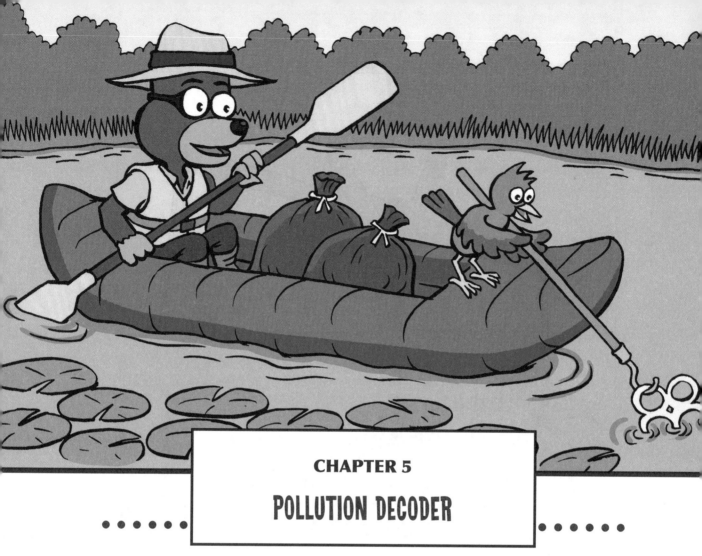

CHAPTER 5

POLLUTION DECODER

When you think of streams and lakes, do you picture a clean smell and healthy wildlife? Or do you see dirty water littered with trash and no water creatures to be found? The goal around the world is healthy, clean waterways. But how does water get dirty in the first place?

There are a few common ways for water to get dirty. Polluted water is not natural. It is often caused by manmade waste or chemicals.

? INVESTIGATE!

What can you do to stop water pollution?

DID YOU KNOW?

United Nations scientists estimate that 80 percent of **wastewater** goes untreated. As the population of the earth grows, water pollution could become an even larger problem.

Sometimes, pollution in the air harms water sources. Chemicals from factories and farms can run off the land into lakes and rivers after a rainfall. Pollutants may even come from your home. When you help your parents wash the car, the soap could end up in a waterway.

And what about wastewater—the dirty water from flushing a toilet, taking a shower, or washing clothes? In some places, the wastewater ends up in a **water treatment plant** so it can get cleaned and reused. In other places, untreated wastewater ends up in waterways. Chemicals and waste in water can be harmful to humans, animals, and plants. Water pollution is a problem all around the world.

GOOD READING!

Chemist Teri Dankovich developed a book printed on filter paper. When you tear out a page and pour water over it, the filter catches 99 percent of all bacteria. The book's pages also have information about clean water printed on them. People in Ghana, Haiti, and India use these books.

Learn more here.

🔍 YOUTUBE DRINKABLE BOOK

THE WATER CYCLE!

THE ALGAE PROBLEM

You might have seen algae on the surface of a lake. These organisms look like blue-green slime. In 2011, a huge mass of algae formed on Lake Erie. The algae blob oozed for more than 10 miles! Scientists blamed the algae mass on a chemical called phosphorus. Phosphorus occurs naturally in lakes, but too much phosphorus makes algae grow rapidly.

Algae, as with all living things, need oxygen to live. Large numbers of algae can use up most of the oxygen in the water. Fish living in water with too much algae won't have enough oxygen and will die off.

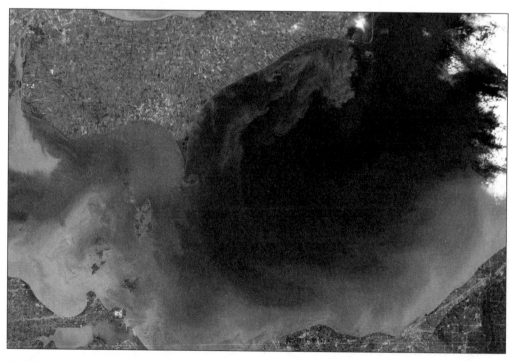

ALGAE ON LAKE ERIE IN 2011

56

The extra phosphorus in Lake Erie came from the surrounding land. Phosphorus is often found in fertilizers used on farms. It can end up in the waterways when rain washes it off the land.

ACID RAIN

The English scientist Robert Angus Smith (1817–1884) was interested in water pollution. In 1852, he came up with the term acid rain for precipitation with high levels of acid.

Scientists measure the amount of acid in rain with the pH scale. A score of zero on the scale is the most acidic. A score of 14.0 is the least acidic. Normal rain has a score between 5.0 and 5.5. Acid rain is about a 4.0.

··· DID YOU KNOW? ···

Scientists have shown that burning fuel is the major cause of acid rain. You can help keep bodies of water clean by using less fuel. Walk or ride your bike to school or use public transportation. Turn off the computer, television, and lights when you are not using them.

GREAT GARBAGE!

Every year, billions of pounds of trash enter the ocean. Some of this trash has become caught in circular ocean currents, forming islands of garbage. The largest garbage patch is in the Pacific Ocean between Hawaii and California. It's called the Great Pacific Garbage Patch and is twice the size of Texas! Researchers with the Ocean Cleanup foundation used planes and ships to measure and study the garbage.

(PS) **Watch a video about how they did this and what they learned.**

🔍 OCEAN CLEANUP GARBAGE PATCH

A STATUE DAMAGED BY ACID RAIN
CREDIT: NINO BARBIERI (CC BY 2.5)

Learn more about acid rain at this website.

🔍 EPA STUDENTS ACID RAIN

Smith believed that coal-burning factories made rain more acidic. Chemicals in the coal, such as sulfuric acid, mixed into the air, changing the pH of the rain.

Acid rain harms the environment. It damages water and soil systems. For example, thousands of lakes around the world are crystal clear and beautiful—and dead. After years of acid rain, these lakes contain no living creatures or plants. The acid rain changed the chemical balance in the soil around the lakes. When the soil couldn't absorb the acid from the rain any longer, the acid flowed into the lakes.

crude oil: thick, natural oil.

OIL SPILL

Each year, **crude oil** leaks into oceans. Most oil leaks are small, but sometimes, they are huge and deadly. On April 20, 2010, a large explosion rocked the Deepwater Horizon oil rig in the Gulf of Mexico. Many workers were injured and 11 people died. The fire on the rig was put out, but deep in the sea, oil began to gush from a pipe connected to the rig. Engineers estimated that every three days, enough oil to fill an Olympic-sized pool escaped into the ocean! The oil harmed many marine animals, including bluefin tuna, dolphins, and sharks. It coated the wings of birds, preventing them from flying. It took people years to clean up the spill.

To solve the acid rain problem, countries work together because pollution travels across borders. In Nova Scotia, Canada, for example, some lakes harmed by acid rain are now recovering. This is because of new rules on coal-burning plants in the United States and Canada.

Even though moving water is a renewable resource, people still need to make sure they don't waste the water they use! In the next chapter, we'll look at the importance of water conservation.

DID YOU KNOW?

In 1972, the U.S. Congress passed the Clean Water Act. It set national standards to protect the health of waterways.

? CONSIDER AND DISCUSS

It's time to consider and discuss: What can you do to stop water pollution?

PROJECT!

WATER IN ROME

SUPPLIES

* scissors
* paper
* pencil
* poster board
* glue
* markers
* 2 to 3 players
* coins
* die

Around 97 CE, the emperor of Rome put an engineer name Julius Frontinus (40–103) in charge of the city's water system. In this board game, help Julius bring a supply of water to Rome.

1 Cut out 20 squares from the paper. Number the squares and write one of the sentences listed on page 61 on each one.

2 Arrange the squares in order on the poster board.

3 Glue each square in place.

4 Decorate the rest of your board with the markers.

To Play:

✳ Use coins as tokens. Each player places a token on the first square, "**1**–Hired!" Players take turns rolling the die. The high roller goes first.

✳ Player No. 1 rolls the die, moves the correct number of spaces, and follows the instructions on the square.

✳ To win, a player must land directly on the last square, "**20**–Rome has water!"

···· DID YOU KNOW?

By 500 BCE, Rome had more than 1,000 fountains. A system of 11 aqueducts carried water into the city.

1
Hired!

2
You are head of the
Roman water supply.

3
Fix an aqueduct,
move ahead two squares.

4
Write a report to the emperor,
roll again.

5
Robbed,
move back to start.

6
Build a public bath,
move ahead one.

7
Fix terracotta pipes,
move ahead two.

8
Public bath breaks,
miss a turn.

9
Workers happy,
move ahead one.

10
Water system mapped,
go to end.

11
Leaks in the system fixed, move
ahead one.

12
Fall while riding through
aqueduct, miss a turn.

13
Visit the emperor,
move ahead one.

14
Day of rest,
miss a turn.

15
Water is stolen,
go back three.

16
Check all systems,
move ahead one.

17
An aqueduct is tapped,
miss a turn.

18
Public fountains run,
roll again.

19
The emperor is pleased,
move ahead one.

20
Rome has water!

OIL SPILL CLEANUP

Scientists use different methods to clean up an oil spill, including skimming oil off the surface and seabed and using chemicals to break up the oil. Try to clean up an oil spill in your kitchen!

1 Pour 2 cups of water into the clear mixing bowl. Add two drops of blue food dye.

2 Slowly pour in ½ cup of vegetable oil.

3 Place the rest of the items on the supply list on the cookie sheet. One by one, use the cotton ball, paper towel, string, sponge, plastic bag, and spoon to try to remove the oil. What happens?

4 Dip the feather in the oil. Try to clean it with detergent. What happens? Record your observations in your journal.

SUPPLIES

* water
* clear mixing bowl
* blue food dye
* ½ cup vegetable oil
* cookie sheet
* cotton ball
* paper towel
* string
* sponge
* plastic bag
* spoon
* feather
* detergent
* science journal and pencil

⋯ DID YOU KNOW? ⋯

A single drop of sea water has millions of bacteria. Some bacteria maybe be able to help scientists clean up oil spills. This is because certain strains of bacteria can break down oil.

TRY THIS! Use cleaners such as shampoo, vinegar, baking soda, and liquid hand soap to clean the oily feather. Which cleaner works best and why?

62

PROJECT!

WATERSHED JOURNEY

SUPPLIES

* ✳ nut, soy, or peanut butter
* ✳ 3 tablespoons honey
* ✳ 1 cup granola
* ✳ mixing bowl
* ✳ ⅓ cup each muesli, shredded coconut, chocolate sprinkles, and raisins
* ✳ 4 paper plates
* ✳ science journal and pencil

A **watershed** is an area of land where rain collects and then drains into a body of water. In this activity, model what a water droplet picks up as it travels through a watershed.

1 Wash your hands, because you'll be working with food.

2 Mix the nut butter, honey, and granola in the bowl. Form bite-sized balls and set aside. These are your raindrops. If the mixture is too wet, spoon in some oats.

3 Place one topping on each plate. The muesli is for leaves, the chocolate sprinkles are for soil, the coconut is for lawn chemicals, the raisins are for detergents. Roll your "raindrops" through the toppings, one by one. How much do your raindrops pick up?

4 After you finished rolling your raindrops, share them with friends!

TRY THIS! With help from an adult, research a watershed in your area. Print out a map and mark its location. Think about all the ways you use the water from the watershed. In your science journal, make a chart showing how you use water within your home. Do you think you use the same amount year-round? Or does your water use change with the seasons? Write down your answer and reasons in your journal.

WORDS TO KNOW

watershed: an area where all the water drains into one river or lake.

CHAPTER 6

WATER WISE

· · · · · · · · · · · · · · · ·

Drip, drip, drip. A leaky tap can waste 24 gallons of water in a day. Do you leave the tap running when you brush your teeth? If so, millions of water molecules go down the drain each time. And every drop counts.

· ·

Even though water never disappears, it can get stuck in ice or underground for thousands of years. That means humans aren't able to drink it, bathe in it, or use it for power. That's why we should all make sure we are using only as much water as we need.

? INVESTIGATE!

What are three ways you can conserve water?

OUT OF WATER

Starting in 2015, the city of Cape Town in South Africa experienced three years of drought. By 2018, the city was in danger of running out of water all together!

The water shortage was so severe that city officials limited residents to 50 liters—about 13 gallons—of water a day. This may seem like a lot of water to you. However, people had to use this water for everything from a quick shower to washing dishes, drinking, cooking, and flushing the toilet. To conserve water, people tried baking or broiling food instead of boiling it. Some people flushed the toilet once a day. People could not water their gardens.

Watch a video timeline about Cape Town's water crisis. What might the city have done differently early on?

🔎 PULITZER CAPE TOWN TIMELINE

The residents of Cape Town were lucky. Eventually, heavy rains boosted the dam levels back up and people were able to use more water. Still, town residents are careful about wasting water!

HOW MUCH WATER?

Toilet flush, 3 gallons

Average bath, 36 gallons

Shower, 2 to 5 gallons per minute

Brushing teeth, 1 gallon

Laundry (1 load), 25 to 40 gallons

The United States is rich in water resources, but this water is not evenly spread out across the country. In Kansas, water levels in the Ogallala Aquifer—a huge underground water reservoir—have dropped 60 percent in the last 60 years. People are using the water that seeps underground from rain or snowmelt faster than it gets replaced. Water shortages could affect farms in the area.

California often experiences droughts. The most recent drought began in 2011. In April 2017, Gov. Jerry Brown announced the drought was over. But two of California's largest reservoirs were still only half full.

Even if your home isn't in South Africa, Kansas, or California, a water shortage could still affect you. Scientists predict that by 2050, almost half of the world's population will not have clean water. We can work now to become more aware about this important resource and how to conserve it.

CONSERVE WATER!

* Turn off the tap when brushing your teeth.
* Keep a jug of water in the fridge instead of running the tap.
* Wash fruits and vegetables in a bowl of water.
* Wash your bike with water from a bucket instead of a hose.

REUSE WATER

Graywater is wastewater from baths, showers, and washing machines that doesn't contain serious contaminants—unlike wastewater from toilets. The average person in the United States produces hundreds of gallons of graywater a year. You can collect graywater and use it to water plants or wash your bike.

BODY OF WATER

Humans need water to live. Tap on your arm, now on your leg. They feel solid, don't they? But did you know water is inside you? Almost 60 percent of your body is water! The body uses water to break down the food you eat. Water also helps rid the body of chemicals and waste it does not need. If you do not drink enough water, your body may become **dehydrated**. Your mouth may feel dry and your head may hurt. You could feel tired or grumpy. To avoid feeling sick, drink water throughout the day. And always drink water after you have played any sports or games to replace the water your body has sweated off. Check out which foods are good to eat for water, too.

FOOD	WATER CONTENT
Cantaloupe	95 percent
Tomato	94 percent
Watermelon	92 percent
Spinach	91 percent
Plain yogurt	88 percent

AQUA MECHANICAL (CC BY 2.0)

People also conserve water by collecting rainwater. Instead of allowing rain to fall freely, they **divert** it from their roofs into large tanks or barrels. Next time it rains, don't let the water fall down the gutter. Collect it! You can use rainwater to water gardens and lawns, wash cars, and clean outdoor furniture.

We've learned a lot about the science of water, but what about the creative side of water? In the next chapter, we'll look at how water has inspired art, music, and more!

? **CONSIDER AND DISCUSS**

It's time to consider and discuss: What three ways could you conserve water in your home?

THEN & NOW

THEN: According to the World Health Organization, more than 260 million people must walk 30 minutes a day to collect safe water. Some carry this heavy load back home on their heads.

NOW: There is a new device to carry clean water called the Hippo Water Roller. It looks like a large barrel. The barrel carries five times as much water as a bucket.

COLLECTING WATER RELAY

In this game, you and your team must run through an obstacle course to collect water. While this is a fun activity, for many people, collecting clean drinking water is not a game.

1 Divide players into two even teams. Set up two identical courses with your obstacles.

2 Place one full bucket of water at the end of each course and one empty bucket at the beginning.

3 The first player from each team grabs a cup, runs through the course, and fills the cup from the end bucket. The player runs back through the course and pours the water into the empty bucket.

4 The player tags the next person and passes the cup. This player runs through the course, fills the cup, runs back to empty it, and passes the cup.

5 The team with the most water in its bucket after five minutes is the winner. What does this show you about water conservation?

WHAT DO YOU CALL A PUDDLE ON A HOT DAY?

Dried Up.

SUPPLIES

* obstacles such as chairs, skipping ropes, or cones
* 4 large buckets
* water
* science journal and pencil

THINK ABOUT IT: In the United States, most people have access to clean water. In your science journal, record how many times you turn on the tap in a day. How long do you keep it running? What do you use this water for? How could you use less?

PROJECT!

RAIN HARVESTER

In North America, some gardeners collect rain in tanks. In parts of Asia, people redirect rain to nearby crops with bamboo. Try this activity to collect and direct water in your garden.

Caution: Standing water can attract mosquitoes. Cover any water container with mesh or cheesecloth.

1 Have an adult help you cut the top and bottom off four water bottles and then cut the bottles in half, lengthwise.

2 Lay the cut bottles out end to end. Join the bottles together using duct tape to make a long channel.

3 Tie the eight sticks together with yarn to form four Xs. Arrange the Xs upright in a line near a garden. The line should be slightly higher at one end. How can you secure the Xs in place?

· · · DID YOU KNOW? · · ·

The state of Florida reuses about 760 million gallons of water each day! The water is used for crops, parks, golf courses, and lawns.

70

CLEAN WATER TECH

There are tiny living things that are too small to see without a microscope. They are called **microorganisms**. Some microorganisms live in water. When people drink water that is not clean, some of these microorganisms can make them ill. **Ultraviolet (UV) light** could help with this problem. It can stop microorganisms from growing in water. Dr. Ashok Gadgil (1950-) invented the UV Waterworks (UVW). His lightweight machine, weighing only 15 pounds, can clean four gallons of water in a minute!

4 Place your water channel on top of the Xs. At the end of the channel, place a container such as a bucket to harvest the rainwater. Or, let the water drain straight into the garden.

5 Pour some water into the channel. Watch how the water flows and write down your observations in your science journal. Add details and diagrams to your notes.

THINK ABOUT IT: Is the water running too quickly or slowly down the channel? What could you change about your design to allow the water to run slower or faster? Write down your ideas and then try them out.

WORDS ⊕ KNOW

microorganism: an organism so small it can be seen only under a microscope.

ultraviolet (UV) light: a kind of light with short wavelengths. It can't be seen with the naked eye.

71

DESIGN A GARDEN

In this activity, create a small garden that uses little water.

1 With help from an adult, research which plants grow well in your area and don't require much water. Your local garden center would be a great place to begin. Write down this information in your science journal.

2 Based on your research, choose up to three plants.

3 Choose an area for your garden near a water source, such as your rain harvester. For a container garden, choose a container made of terracotta or wood. These materials hold water longer.

4 If you are not using a container, decide on a shape for your garden, perhaps a raindrop or circle. Use the spade to dig out this shape.

PROJECT!

Xeriscaping is gardening with plants that need little water. In this type of landscaping, people also use shredded wood, leaves, or gravel to cover garden beds. When soil is protected from the sun, less water evaporates into the air. **Learn more at this website.**

🔍 CLIMATE KIDS LANDSCAPER ⎯ ⎯ ⎯ ⎯ ⎯ ⎯ ⎯ ⎯ →

5 Pull out any grass or weeds. Add a little compost to help the soil hold moisture.

6 Follow the planting instructions and then soak the soil with water. Cover the soil with mulch to prevent the water from evaporating.

7 During the next few weeks, write down your observations in your science journal. Why do you think **native** plants usually need less care than plants from other areas?

> **TRY THIS!** If you planted a garden in the sun, try one in the shade. Do you think this will change your results? Try it and see.

WORDS TO KNOW

xeriscaping: landscaping with rocks and plants that need very little or no water.

native: a plant or animal that is naturally found in a certain area.

73

CHAPTER 7

WATER INNOVATIONS

Water is a clear liquid with no taste, smell, or color. But did you know that water is also a source of ideas? Water inspires musicians, artists, and scientists to create sounds, images, and machines. We also celebrate water with festivals and events.

It's interesting to think of water as being part of the culture beyond the role it plays in keeping us and the environment healthy. Let's learn more.

 INVESTIGATE!

What kind of creations does water inspire?

WATER INSTRUMENTS

The ancient Greeks invented the hydraulis, an instrument powered by water. Air was forced through a container of water. Sound came from long, flute-like pipes along the top of the instrument. The instrument was so popular that it was played at theaters and fairs.

hydraulis: the earliest known mechanical pipe organ.

armonica: a musical instrument invented by Ben Franklin in 1761. It is played by rubbing wet fingers against a set of turning, crystal bowls.

percussion: a musical instrument that is played by hitting or shaking.

WORDS ᴛᴏ KNOW

WHAT DID THE PUDDLE SAY TO THE RAINDROP?

Drop by anytime!

Much later, American inventor Benjamin Franklin (1706–1790) became interested in the sound of water in glass. Have you ever run wet fingers around the edge of a glass of water? When you rub the rim, you create a ringing sound.

Franklin wanted to capture this sound in an instrument. He attached 37 glass bowls of water to a spindle and a foot pedal. When he pressed the pedal, the bowls spun and Franklin rubbed his fingers around their rims. He called this new instrument an armonica. Its delicate sound became very popular.

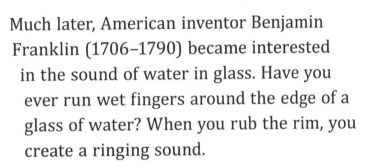

PS Tan Dun (1957–) is a Chinese composer and conductor. Dun's *Water Concerto* blends **percussion** instruments and water. Musicians pour water from one container to another. They move their hands around the edges of large, water-filled bowls. They pour water through kitchen strainers to create sounds like a waterfall. **Listen to Tan Dun's music at this website.**

🔍 TAN DUN WATER MUSIC

WATER LILIES BY CLAUDE MONET, 1916

ART AND ARCHITECTURE

Water inspires artists and architects. The French artist Claude Monet (1840–1926) spent many hours painting by his lily pond. As the hours passed from sunrise to dusk, Monet noticed how the beauty of the pond shifted as the light changed. In each painting he did of the pond, his brushstrokes and paint colors changed to capture the changes of light on the water.

Frank Lloyd Wright (1867–1959) was a famous American architect. In 1934, he created a daring design in Pennsylvania. His client wanted him to build a home near a waterfall. Wright created a design around the natural landscape. He wanted his client to feel as if he was part of the waterfall. This home is known as Fallingwater.

FALLINGWATER, A HOUSE DESIGNED BY ARCHITECT FRANK LLOYD WRIGHT IN PENNSYLVANIA

NATURE-INSPIRED WATER SCIENCE

Biomimicry is the science of creating **technology** based on ideas from nature. In Latin, *bios* means "life" and *mimesis* means "to copy." Inspired by nature, scientists are working on exciting new products.

The bioWAVE is an 85-foot-high machine designed to collect the energy from waves and convert it into electricity. Engineers based their design on seaweed. Like seaweed, the bioWAVE moves underwater in response to the movement of waves. Energy from the waves is converted to electricity.

Engineers are testing the machine in Australia. In the future, this technology might be able to supply people with low-cost, clean energy.

> **biomimicry:** the science of creating technology based on ideas from nature.
>
> **technology:** the tools, methods, and systems used to solve a problem or do work.
>
> **WORDS ⊙ KNOW**

WATER TRIKE

Innovate or Die is a competition that challenges college students to come up with solutions to real-life problems. In 2008, students were asked to build a machine that could help people carry and clean water. The winning entry was the Aquaduct—a large blue tricycle with water tanks. The Aquaduct not only transported water, but also filtered and cleaned it while the rider pedaled!

 PS Watch a video about the Aquaduct vehicle at this website.

🔍 INNOVATE OR DIE AQUADUCT

THE WATER CYCLE!

(PS) Scroll through the home page on this site to see some images of the AquaWeb.

─ ─ ─ ─ ─ →

🔍 AQUAWEB

To provide sustainable water to farmers in cities, a company called NexLoop created a remarkable product. The AquaWeb is a water system based on an orb spider's web. The system captures moisture from the air just as an orb spider collects water in a web. Water is stored in blocks in the AquaWeb's honeycomb. The blocks can be used in greenhouses.

CELEBRATE!

We celebrate water around the world in many different ways. In Cambodia, a three-day water festival called Bon Om Touk marks the end of the rainy season. People hold longboat races and set off fireworks.

Songkran is a festival held each April in Thailand, Cambodia, and Laos. It's a three-day water fight! Children and adults use buckets, cups, water soakers, and water balloons to spray water all over the place. People believe that the water will wash away their bad luck.

You've learned a lot about why water is important to life on Earth. You've also learned how human activity affects water and how people are working to protect it. If you set an example by taking care of water resources, your efforts could become a new water celebration that spreads across your region, country, or the world!

CONSIDER AND DISCUSS

It's time to consider and discuss: What kind of creations does water inspire?

SUPPLIES
* science journal and pencil
* pencil crayons

BIOMIMICRY WATER STORAGE

Some animals can live without water for years! Giant tortoises on the Galápagos Islands store water in their bladders and can live on it for up to a year during times of little rain. A cactus can live in a dry desert because it uses its long roots to collect and store water. In this activity, design a water holder inspired by a plant or an animal.

1 With help from an adult, research one desert animal or plant. Head to the library for help!

2 In your journal, write down how it collects and stores water. Add pictures.

3 Design a water holder based on this animal or plant.

4 Draw a picture of your invention and add labels to it. How would you encourage people to use your design?

DID YOU KNOW?

Approximately 20 percent of all water waste in the world is due to leaky pipes. A team of engineers based in Boston, Massachusetts, tackled this problem, building a robot that can sense water leaks. They took inspiration from aquatic creatures such as the blind cave fish, which senses changes in water pressure.

TRY THIS! Build a prototype of your water holder using materials you have in your house. Does your design work? How can you improve it?

WORDS TO KNOW

prototype: a working model of something that lets engineers test their idea.

79

PROJECT!

MAKE A BUDDHA BOARD

Have fun and express yourself with a Buddha Board. You don't need paint, because the board only needs a brush, water, and your imagination.

SUPPLIES

* natural or white picture frame
* 2–4 colors of craft paint
* paper plate
* foam board
* pencil
* scissors
* Mod Podge (1 cup white glue and ⅓ cup water)
* foam brush
* magic water painting paper or similar
* cup of water
* paintbrush

1 Remove the back from the photo frame and set it aside. Ask an adult to remove the glass. You will not be needing it for this project.

2 Pour a little of each paint color on the paper plate. Dip your finger into the first color and press onto the frame. Allow each color to dry before applying the next color. Set your painted frame to one side and allow it to dry completely.

3 Now, place the back of the photo frame on top of the foam board and trace around it. Do the same for the magic water painting paper.

4 Cut out the foam board and the paper. Set the paper to one side. Use the sponge brush to spread the Mod Podge on the top of the foam board. Place the paper on the foam board and press to eliminate air bubbles.

5 Place the foam board into your frame. Replace the frame back and secure. Your Buddha Board is ready to be used.

6 Place your Buddha Board on a flat surface. To draw a picture, take the brush and dip it into the cup of water. What will you create?

PROJECT!

GUESS THE SOUND

Collect water sounds and have your friends guess what they are in this fun activity.

> **Before using any app, ask an adult for permission.**

SUPPLIES

* A free audio recording app such as Vocaroo or SpeakPipe
* water tap
* different size plastic and metal bowls
* strainer
* paper and ceramic cups
* jug
* foil pan
* baking tin
* cardboard
* science journal and pencil

1 Have your audio recording app ready. Arrange your materials from the supply list near a tap.

2 Start recording and pour the water from one object to another. Pour the water slowly, quickly, and from different heights. Write down the order in which you created your sounds in your journal. Write down any other observations.

3 Fill a sink and use your fingers to move the water. How many sounds can you create? If you are using a mobile device, try recording water sounds outdoors, such as the sound of water coming out of a hose or dripping from a roof.

4 Invite friends to listen to the sounds you recorded. Can they guess what they are? Without looking in your journal, ask a friend to play the recording for you. Can you guess the sounds correctly?

> **TRY THIS!** Create music with your recorded water sounds. Use an instrument, clap your hands, or make simple instruments to accompany what you recorded. For example, a few sprinkles or beans in an empty plastic bottle makes a great shaker.

MAKE AND PLAY A WATER XYLOPHONE

In this activity, experiment with water-filled glasses to make music. Maybe you will design a new musical instrument as Benjamin Franklin did!

SUPPLIES

* 6 identical glass bottles
* circle stickers and marker
* measuring jug
* water
* spoon or wood stick

1 Line up the bottles on a flat surface. Write the numbers 1 through 6 on the circle stickers. Attach one sticker to each bottle.

2 Use the jug to pour a different amount of water into each bottle. Bottle 1 will have the most water. Bottle 2 will have a little less, and so on, until all bottles are filled.

3 Gently strike each bottle with the spoon and listen carefully to the sound. Adjust the amount of water in each bottle until they sound like a musical scale. What do you notice about the amount of water in a bottle and the sound it makes?

TRY THIS! Try and play a simple song or compose your own music.

MUSIC INSPIRED BY WATER

Water has inspired composers and musicians throughout history. George Frideric Handel (1685–1759) composed a famous piece called *Water Music*—to be played on water! In 1717, *Water Music* was played on the Thames River in London for King George I (1660–1727), who listened to the music from a boat.

acid rain: precipitation that has been polluted by acid.

adapt: to make a change in response to new or different conditions.

algae: simple organisms found in water that are like plants but without roots, stems, or leaves.

anemometer: a weather instrument that measures wind speed.

aquatic: living or growing in water.

aqueduct: a network of channels used to move water across long distances.

aquifer: an underground layer of rock that has space in it that holds water.

armonica: a musical instrument invented by Ben Franklin in 1761. It is played by rubbing wet fingers against a set of turning, crystal bowls.

atmosphere: a layer of gases around the earth.

atom: the smallest particle of matter.

axle: a rod on which a wheel rotates.

barometer: a weather instrument that measures air pressure.

biomimicry: the science of creating technology based on ideas from nature.

capillary action: the way water pulls itself up into another material.

cargo: things carried by ship, truck, train, or airplane.

cistern: an underground well used for storing water.

climate: the average weather patterns in an area during a long period of time.

climate change: changes in the earth's climate patterns, including rising temperatures, which is called global warming.

collection: the process by which water that falls back to the earth is stored on land or in oceans, ponds, rivers, lakes, and streams.

condensation: the process by which a gas cools and forms a liquid.

conservation: managing and protecting natural resources.

conserve: to use something carefully, so it isn't used up.

contaminant: a material that makes something dirty or unfit for use.

continent: a large landmass.

crop: a plant grown for food or other uses.

crude oil: thick, natural oil.

culture: the beliefs and customs of a group of people.

current: the constant movement of water in a direction.

dam: a large, strong wall built across a river to hold back and control the water.

dehydrated: suffering from a great loss of water in the body.

dense: tightly packed.

dew: water droplets made when humid air cools at night.

diameter: the distance across a circle through the middle.

divert: to change course or turn from one direction to another.

drought: a long period of little or no rain.

ecosystem: a community of plants and animals living in an area and relying on each other to survive.

element: a substance that contains only one kind of atom.

engineer: a person who uses science, math, and creativity to design and build things.

engineering: the use of science, math, and creativity in the design and construction of things.

equator: an invisible line circling the globe, halfway between the North and South Poles.

erosion: the wearing down of the earth's surface, usually by water, wind, or ice.

evaporation: the process by which a liquid becomes a gas.

fossil fuel: a fuel such as oil, coal, or natural gas, which takes millions of years to form from the remains of plant and animals.

generator: a machine that converts energy into electricity.

glacier: a huge mass of ice and snow.

global conveyor belt: a constantly moving system of circulating water in the ocean that helps regulate temperature and salt levels.

gravity: a force that pulls all objects to the earth.

THE WATER CYCLE!

graywater: water that was used for activities such as laundry or washing dishes.

greenhouse gas: a gas in the atmosphere that traps heat.

groundwater: water found in the soil in the spaces between rocks.

humidity: the amount of moisture in the air.

hydraulis: the earliest known mechanical pipe organ.

hydroelectric: electricity generated by waterpower.

hydrogen: the most common element in the universe, and one of the elements of water.

hydrologist: a person who studies water.

hydropower: energy produced by the movement of water.

hygrometer: an instrument that measures humidity.

ice age: a period in time when the earth cools down and ice spreads over a large part of the planet.

ice cap: a thick layer of permanent ice.

ice sheet: a thick layer of ice covering a large area of land for a long time, especially those in Antarctica and Greenland.

irrigation: a system of transporting water through canals or tunnels to water crops.

landform: a physical feature of the earth's surface, such as a mountain or a valley.

lever: a bar that rests on a support and lifts or moves things.

matter: any material or substance that takes up space.

meteorologist: a scientist who studies weather and makes predictions about it.

meteorology: the study of weather and climate.

microorganism: an organism so small it can be seen only under a microscope.

minerals: naturally occurring solids found in rocks and in the ground.

molecule: a group of atoms.

native: a plant or animal that is naturally found in a certain area.

nilometer: a device used in ancient Egypt to measure the height of water reached by the Nile during its annual floods.

organism: any living thing, such as a plant or animal.

oxygen: an element that is a gas in the air. People and animals need oxygen to live.

percussion: a musical instrument that is played by hitting or shaking.

phosphorus: a chemical known to pollute waterways.

pH scale: a scale that measures acids.

pollute: to make dirty or unclean with chemicals or other waste.

pothole: a pond that forms in a natural hollow in the ground.

precipitation: water that falls back to the earth's surface as rain, snow, or hail.

prototype: a working model of something that lets engineers test their idea.

qanat: an underground water tunnel.

radar: a device that detects objects by bouncing radio waves off them and measuring how long it takes for the waves to return.

radiosonde: a small, lightweight box with weather instruments and a radio transmitter.

renewable: something that can be replaced after we use it.

reservoir: a place that holds water.

resource: something found in nature that is useful to humans, such as water to drink, trees to burn, and fish to eat.

rotation: a turn around a fixed point.

runoff: the flow of water that drains off an area of land.

saturated zone: an area below ground filled with water.

sediment: bits of rock, sand, or dirt that have been carried to a place by water, wind, or a glacier.

shaduf: a water-lifting device.

species: a group of plants or animals that are closely related and produce offspring.

stomata: the tiny openings on plant leaves for air to enter.

surface tension: the force that holds the molecules together on the surface of a liquid, so that the liquid acts like it has a stretchy skin. Water has a high surface tension.

technology: the tools, methods, and systems used to solve a problem or do work.

terrarium: a sealed, transparent container in which plants are grown.

tide: the daily rise and fall of the ocean's water level near a shore.

transpiration: the process by which a plant pulls water up through its roots, which then collects on its leaves and evaporates into the atmosphere.

turbine: a machine with rotating blades that changes one type of energy into another.

ultraviolet (UV) light: a kind of light with short wavelengths. It can't be seen with the naked eye.

unsaturated zone: an area below ground that has water and air between rocks.

wastewater: dirty water that has been used by people in their homes, in factories, and in other businesses.

water cycle: the continuous movement of water from the earth to the clouds and back to earth again.

watershed: an area where all the water drains into one river or lake.

water treatment plant: a place where wastewater is cleaned.

water vapor: water in the form of a gas, such as steam or mist.

waterway: a channel of water, such as a stream or river.

water wheel: a wheel with paddles attached that spins when water flows over it. The energy can be used to power machines or lift water.

weather balloon: a special kind of balloon that carries instruments into the atmosphere to take measurements.

wetland: a low area filled with water, such as a marsh or swamp.

xeriscaping: landscaping with rocks and plants that need very little or no water.

METRIC CONVERSIONS

Use this chart to find the metric equivalents to the English measurements in this book. If you need to know a half measurement, divide by two. If you need to know twice the measurement, multiply by two. How do you find a quarter measurement? How do you find three times the measurement?

English	Metric
1 inch	2.5 centimeters
1 foot	30.5 centimeters
1 yard	0.9 meter
1 mile	1.6 kilometers
1 pound	0.5 kilogram
1 teaspoon	5 milliliters
1 tablespoon	15 milliliters
1 cup	237 milliliters

BOOKS

Donovan, Emily. *Exploring Earth's Water Cycle.* Rosen Publishing Group, 2019.

Paul, Miranda, and Jason Chin. *Water Is Water: A Book About the Water Cycle.* Roaring Brook Press, 2015.

Latham, Donna. *Oceans.* Nomad Press, 2010.

Maloof, Torrey. *Water Cycle.* Teacher Created Materials, 2014.

Olien, Rebecca Jean. *The Water Cycle at Work.* Capstone Press, 2016.

Ransom, Candice. *Investigating the Water Cycle.* Lerner, 2017.

Robertson, Joanne. *The Water Walker.* Second Story Press, 2017.

Strauss, Rochelle, and Rosemary Woods. *One Well: The Story of Water on Earth.* Kids Can Press, 2007.

Verde, Susan, and Georgie Badiel. *The Water Princess.* G.P. Putnam's Sons Books for Young Readers, 2016.

Yasuda, Anita. *Oceans and Seas! With 25 Science Projects for Kids.* Nomad Press, 2018.

MUSEUMS AND SCIENCE CENTERS

American Museum of Natural History, New York, New York
amnh.org/exhibitions/water

Arizona Science Center, Phoenix, Arizona
azscience.org

California Science Center, Los Angeles, California
californiasciencecenter.org

The Carnegie Science Museum, Pittsburgh, Pennsylvania
carnegiesciencecenter.org

Connecticut Science Center, Hartford, Connecticut
ctsciencecenter.org

The Franklin Institute, Philadelphia, Pennsylvania
fi.edu

Miami Science Museum, Miami, Florida
miamisci.org

Orpheum Children's Science Museum, Champaign, Illinois
orpheumkids.com

Scripps Institution of Oceanography, San Diego, California
scripps.ucsd.edu

Virginia Institute of Marine Science, Gloucester Point, Virginia
vims.edu

WEBSITES

Brain Pop – Water Cycle
brainpop.com/search/?keyword=Water+Cycle

EPA Learning and Teaching about the Environment
epa.gov/kids/water.htm

EPA Water Sense for Kids
epa.gov/watersense/watersense-kids

Family Education: Water Conservation Tips for Kids
familyeducation.com/life/going-green/earthsavers-water-conservation-tips-kids

Ferguson Foundation – Water Cycle
fergusonfoundation.org/?s=water+cycle

NASA Climate Kids
climatekids.nasa.gov/water-cycle

National Geographic Kids – Water Cycle
kids.nationalgeographic.com/explore/science/water-cycle

PBS Water Cycle Animation
pbslearningmedia.org/resource/ess05.sci.ess.watcyc.watercycle/water-cycle-animation

Planet Pals World Water Day
planetpals.com/world-water-day.htm

United Nations – Water News
unwater.org/news/un-water-news

USGS Water Science
usgs.gov/special-topic/water-science-school

Virtual Koshland Science Museum – Safe Drinking Water
koshland-science-museum.org/water/new

Water Footprint Calculator
watercalculator.org/education/water-resources-for-educators

Water Use It Wisely
wateruseitwisely.com/kids/index.php

Weather Wiz Kids
weatherwizkids.com

ESSENTIAL QUESTIONS

Introduction: What are some differences between fresh water and salt water?

Chapter 1: How does water change from a solid to a liquid to a gas?

Chapter 2: What are clouds made of?

Chapter 3: How are weather and water connected?

Chapter 4: What are some ways humans control water?

Chapter 5: What can you do to stop water pollution?

Chapter 6: What are three ways you can conserve water?

Chapter 7: What kind of creations does water inspire?

QR CODE GLOSSARY